First published 2025 by University of Queensland Press
PO Box 6042, St Lucia, Queensland 4067 Australia

University of Queensland Press (UQP) acknowledges the Traditional Owners and their custodianship of the lands on which UQP operates. We pay our respects to their Ancestors and their descendants, who continue cultural and spiritual connections to Country. We recognise their valuable contributions to Australian and global society.

uqp.com.au
reception@uqp.com.au

Cover and internal design by Stephanie Spartels
Colour reproduction by Splitting Image
Photograph of Molly Hunt by Tim Lanzon
Printed in China by 1010 Printing International

The mural depicted on pages 18–19 is *Birin-birin (Rainbow Bee-eater)* by Narelda's eldest daughter, Jade Dolman, aka JD Penangke. Reproduced with permission of the artist.

University of Queensland Press is supported by the Queensland Government through Arts Queensland.

University of Queensland Press is assisted by the Australian Government through Creative Australia, its principal arts investment and advisory body.

A catalogue record for this book is available from the National Library of Australia.

ISBN 978 0 7022 6921 9 (hbk)

IF QUEERS WEREN'T MEANT TO HAVE KIDS...

Narelda Jacobs & Karina Natt
Illustrated by Molly Hunt

If queers weren't meant to have kids ...
U-HAUL

... why do lesbians nest after one week?

If queers weren't meant to have kids ...

... why were turkey basters invented?

If queers weren't meant to have kids ...
HEY DADDY!

... why are hot gays called daddy?

If queers weren't meant to have kids ...
Mother Tucker!

... why are drag queens so maternal?

If queers weren't meant to have kids ...

... why is the village full of babysitters?

If queers weren't meant to have kids ...

... would anyone be born?

If queers weren't meant to have kids ...

FERTILITY CLINIC

START YOUR FAMILY WITH U$

LGBTIQ+ FERTILITY & IVF
We'll help you start your Rainbow Family
... why do IVF clinics take the pink dollar?

If queers weren't meant to have kids ...

CLOSE THE BOOK ON DRAG STORYTIME

HELL IS WAITING FOR YOU!

PUBLIC LIBRARIES FOR EDUCATION NOT INDOCTRINATION

GOD WILL BE THE JUDGE

PUBLIC LIBRARY
5G CAUSES COVID
THE EARTH
s FLAT
THERE'S ONLY 2 Genders
... what else would culture war conservatives do with their time?
Poisoning Children

If queers weren't meant to have kids ...

... why are their children so successful?

If queers weren't meant to have kids ...

... why aren't their children ever an accident?

If queers weren't meant to have kids ...
RAINBOW FAMILY

... why can they?

Narelda Jacobs OAM is a Whadjuk Noongar journalist, presenter, commentator and keynote speaker. Starting in the Perth newsroom in 2000, Narelda's career at Network 10 has spanned a quarter of a century and seen her present daily national news bulletins, current affairs shows and lifestyle programs.

Karina Natt is a former lawyer and journalist who spent a decade working as a senior adviser in federal politics. Karina is now working in communications and media production and advisory. Together with Narelda, she is working to elevate First Nations and queer voices across platforms.

Molly Hunt is a multitalented Balanggarra and Yolngu artist from Wyndham, Kimberley, Western Australia. Her blend of digital illustrations, animations and mural art has resulted in collaborations with major brands such as The Body Shop, Google, TikTok and FIFA. In 2023, with DeadlyScience founder Corey Tutt, Molly published *This Book Thinks Ya Deadly!*, an illustrated compendium that celebrates the diversity and success of First Nations people.